NATURE'S LIGHT

By the Same Author
The Freshwater Eel
Sea Turtles

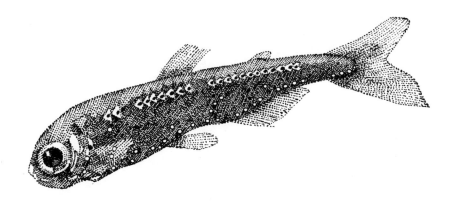

Francine Jacobs
NATURE'S
LIGHT
The Story of
Bioluminescence

ILLUSTRATED BY PAMELA CARROLL

William Morrow and Company

New York 1974

The author wishes to thank Dr. J. Woodland Hastings, Professor of Biology at Harvard University, for reading and checking the manuscript of this book.

Library of Congress Cataloging in Publication Data

Jacobs, Francine.
  Nature's light: the story of bioluminescence.

  SUMMARY: Describes the plants and animals that glow with their own light and discusses what scientists have discovered about this phenomenon and its possible uses.
  1. Bioluminescence — Juvenile literature.
  [1. Bioluminescence] I. Carroll, Pamela, illus.
  II. Title.
  QH641.J3   574.1'9125   73-18326
  ISBN 0-688-20115-6
  ISBN 0-688-30115-0 (lib. bdg.)

"Wishes are secrets hanging on the end of wishbones, hiding behind the new moon, sparkling on the tip of a star." *The Wisher's Handbook*

For Jean Fritz,
who helped a wish come true.

CONTENTS

NATURE'S LIGHT

Around the earth, living on the land and in the seas, are strange creatures that glow by their own light. These very different animals and some simple plants, too, share the wonder of nature's light: bioluminescence. *Bio* means from living things, and *luminescence* is light produced at low temperatures.

Thousands of visitors come to a cave in New Zealand to marvel at the twinkling lights of tiny glistening worms. Along riverbanks in Thailand, blinking fireflies cling to the leaves of trees, flashing on and off like the lights on a Christmas tree. In the dark depths of the sea, where food is scarce, the angler fish catches its dinner by attracting it with a glowing lure. In many places, on summer nights, fireflies catch our attention by flickering their colored lanterns.

Bioluminescence is more common among animals than it is among plants. There are some forty orders of animals, each of which has at least one species, or member, that produces light. Most of them are simple creatures, like earthworms, insects, and jellyfishes. The fishes are the only luminescent animals advanced enough to have backbones. No amphibians, reptiles, birds, or mammals light up.

Thailand fireflies create a tropical Christmas tree.

Nature's light has fascinated man for ages, but bioluminescence remained merely a curiosity until recent developments. Now science is learning the secrets of this mysterious cold light and putting it to use. What are these odd creatures that light up?

ON THE LAND

The New Zealand Glowworm

Can you imagine the awe of the first New Zealanders who entered Waitomo Cave? Above them the ceiling shimmered with thousands of tiny, bluish-white lights that looked like sparkling stars in the night sky. Perhaps they gasped or called out to a companion. Any sound

New Zealand glowworm

would have plunged the cave into darkness as if someone had pulled a switch. A cough, even a whisper, frightens these New Zealand glow-worms and causes them to turn off their lights at once. Guides caution the thousands of tourists who visit Waitomo today to keep still, or else they too may be left in the dark.

The mysterious lights of Waitomo are glowing inch-long worms, the immature larval form of flies. They hang from the roof of the grotto in transparent tubes, trying to lure flying insects onto sticky threads that they suspend below them like flypaper. Once caught, the insect is reeled up, and the worm has his meal.

Fireflies

In Thailand, fireflies of the species *Pteroptyx malaccae* put on unusual, spectacular eye-catching displays. In the daytime, like all fireflies, *Pteroptyx* remains under shady cover. But as

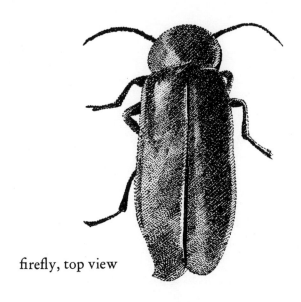

firefly, top view

night approaches the males come out of hiding and gather on the leaves of certain trees along riverbanks. Suddenly a group of fireflies flash. Other groups take up the signal, and soon all the branches and all the trees are flashing on and off together in unison.

The purpose of this group flashing may be courtship. The males cluster together combining

firefly, bottom view

their lights to better advertise their where-abouts. Singly, their small individual lights would be lost among the dense foliage in these swampy, jungle areas. "Firefly" trees can be seen flashing in the dark from half a mile away. Night after night all throughout the year this dramatic performance goes on in the tropics, where fireflies mate continuously.

No luminescent creature has been studied more than the common firefly, or "lightning bug." It is found everywhere except the continent of Antarctica. As long as 3000 years ago, the ancient Chinese wrote about fireflies and may be responsible for the earliest scientific description of them. About 100 B.C. they classified them as winged insects with fire in

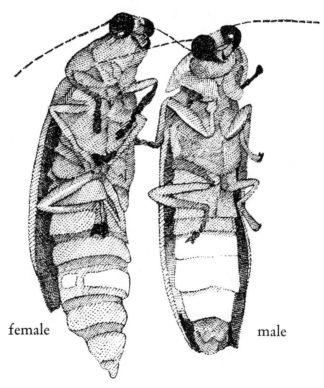

female   male

fireflies showing lighted segments

their body. Somewhat more than a hundred years later on the other side of the world, fireflies also interested the great Roman naturalist, Pliny the Elder.

Pliny mistakenly believed that the firefly's light is controlled by its wings and that it lights up only when its wings are spread. Today we know that chemical impulses control the light. Some fireflies, in fact, have no wings at all and never fly. Among certain European species, females are wingless and are called glowworms. The larval stage of the firefly also is often referred to as the glowworm. Actually the firefly, or glowworm, is neither a fly nor a worm, but is correctly classified as a beetle. Flies have only two wings, while fireflies and other beetles have four. The firefly has two front wings, which are leathery and mainly protective, and two delicate hind wings for flying. The firefly's lights are in its tail.

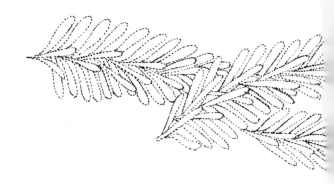

Just as each type of bird has its own particular song, each kind of firefly has its own special pattern of lighting. The lights vary in color from the common yellow to orange. They also vary in the time interval between flashes. Fireflies flash their lights in a kind of Morse code to court mates only of their own species. There is, however, an exception. The female of the species *Photuris pennsylvanica,* found from Massachusetts to Panama, imitates the lighting pattern of a *Photinus scintillans* firefly. She lures the male *Photinus* to her, but not to mate. She prefers to eat him.

common North American firefly
(*Photuris pennsylvanica*)

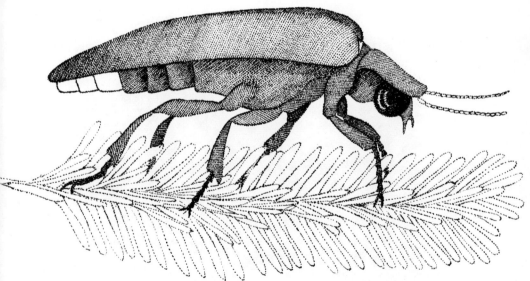

Photinus pyralis is the common North American firefly found from New York to northern Florida and from Kansas to the east coast. The male flies through the air flashing his yellow beacon for one half second. The female, which generally waits on the ground or on a blade of grass, pauses two seconds before flashing back her response. On warm evenings she answers slightly sooner, and on cool nights a little later. The fireflies signal back and forth to one another until the male finally locates the waiting female and joins her to mate.

Male and female fireflies signal to one another.

If you should want to attract a male *Photinus pyralis,* shine a small penlight near the ground for half a second. When a male responds, wait two seconds before answering. Continue carefully in this pattern until he approaches. As he draws near push the tip of your light into the ground to dim it, because an actual female *Photinus* dims her light as the male flies toward her.

The Fire Beetle

An unusually large firefly is the fire beetle, *Pyrophorus,* found on the islands in the Caribbean Sea. It is one of the click beetles, so named because it makes a clicking sound with its back. Unlike the common firefly, which is about half an inch or less in length, *Pyrophorus* often grows to two inches. It has a flickering, heart-shaped orange light on its abdomen that can be seen only when the beetle is in flight. Its main lights, however, are two large, round greenish-yellow ones located on either side of its back just behind the head. They may stay lighted for minutes at a time. These front lights so resemble the switched-on headlights of an automobile that *Pyrophorus* is also called the "automobile bug." Five of them provide enough light to read by.

The fire beetle may have changed the history of the New World. In 1634, when the English were about to land at night on the island of

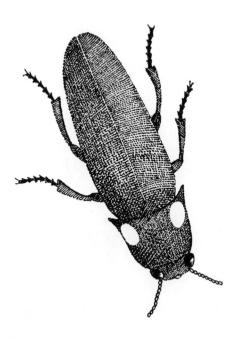

Cuba, they saw many lights. Mistakenly, they believed them to be torches held by Spanish forces already on the island. Deciding that they were greatly outnumbered, the English withdrew and sailed on. What they probably observed were the glowing lights of fire beetles.

The Railroad Worm

In South and Central America there lives a curious cousin of the firefly. It is a beetle whose tongue twister of a name is *Phrixothrix*. The larval form and the adult female light up at night in two colors if stimulated. These creatures, which resemble worms, have two red headlights that glow like burning coals and eleven pairs of greenish-yellow lanterns along the sides of their body. They may shine all or any number of their lights at a time. When totally lighted, the worm, which may attain two inches in length in its wingless adult female form, looks like a tiny passenger train wending its way through the night. For this reason, it is called *"el ferrocarril,"* the Spanish words for *railroad.*

IN THE SEA

Dinoflagellates

The sea, from its surface down into the dark depths, has many more of nature's lights than exist on the land. In the Caribbean Sea, on the southwest coast of the island of Puerto Rico, there is a bay with a ghostly light that can be seen on any night of the year. It is particularly

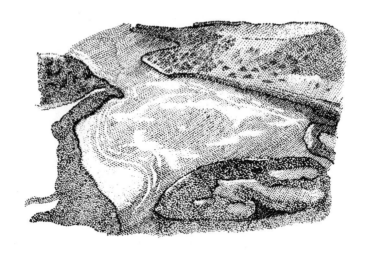

eerie on dark, moonless nights. This place is
Bahía Fosforescente, Phosphorescent Bay. Its
waters shimmer with a greenish-white light,
which flashes only when the surface is disturbed
by the wind, waves, fishes, or boats. At night a
swimmer glows with a ghostly greenish "fire."
So bright is this light that you easily could
read your watch or take a picture in it. Should
you run your hand slowly through the water,
you would see countless tiny sparklers.

Responsible for this strange night light are billions of yellowish, one-celled plants called "dinoflagellates," which flash and whip about on threadlike tails. Dinoflagellates are found lighting up the waters of other bays throughout the world. The seas almost everywhere display

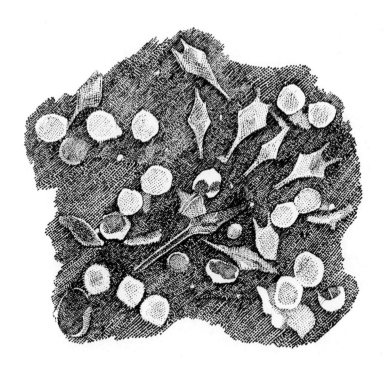

dinoflagellate bioluminescence, especially in late summer when these simple organisms flourish.

The Sea Firefly

In the shallow, coastal waters around Japan, there lives a luminescent creature, no larger than a cucumber seed, that looks like a tiny clam with a transparent shell. It bears the scientific name, *Cypridina.* In the daytime, *Cypridina* remains in the sandy bottom, but at night, using tiny side legs with which to swim, it rises to the surface to feed. If disturbed, it leaves behind a trail of bright blue light. For this reason, the Japanese call *Cypridina* the "sea firefly."

This tiny crustacean was taken on secret military missions. During the Second World War, the Japanese gathered *Cypridina* by the bushel for their soldiers out in the jungles.

Instead of using flashlights or lighting matches, which might have been seen by the enemy, Japanese soldiers used crushed and moistened *Cypridina* in the palms of their hands to light up their maps and orders. Amazingly, powdered *Cypridina,* when moistened, will still shine even after twenty-five years.

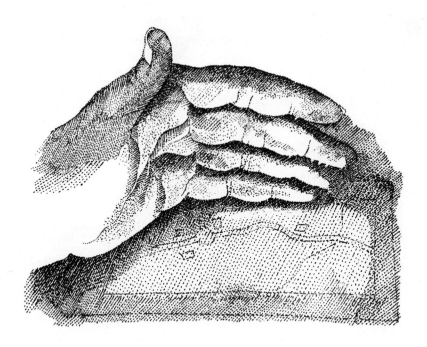

The Fireworm

In the sea there are creatures also that seem to use light to attract mates. Of them, perhaps none is more extraordinary than the Bermuda fireworm, *Odontosyllis.* This animal is so remarkable that Christopher Columbus took time to describe it in his ship's log. In 1492, on the night before Columbus landed on the island of San Salvador in the New World, he wrote of a phenomenon that looked like "moving candles in the sea."

This strange occurrence was undoubtedly the spectacular mating performance of the marine fireworm. Only on three or four nights, after the full moon and about fifty-five minutes past sunset, is the unusual rite observed. The female worm rises from her home in the coral reefs to the surface of the sea, glowing brightly. She swims round and round in circles, emitting a bluish glow. Her lights may attract one or a

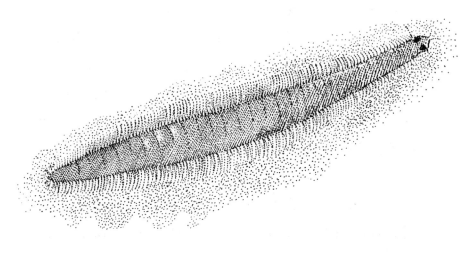

number of male fireworms, which also surface
and flash their lights. An exciting show begins.
For fifteen to thirty minutes, the worms, like
"moving candles," light up the sea. Swimming
in circles, the female gives off a luminous fluid
that contains eggs to which the male adds sperm
and, thus, fertilizes them.

The Firefly Squid

Like the firefly and fireworm, the squid, *Watasenia scintillans,* also uses light to find a mate. This species is named for the Japanese biologist, Watase, who identified it. The four-inch-long squid is seen lighting up the waters along the west coast of Japan in the springtime. It comes to the surface of the sea at night and swims about flashing tiny blue-white lights like stars all over its body. In this way, it attracts mates; it also attracts fishermen. Flat-bottomed boats, often containing as many as forty men, women and children, set forth to catch these squid. When the squid shine, the fishermen scoop them up in dip nets. Later these firefly squid provide a tasty treat. They are eaten fried, broiled, or boiled—lights and all.

In daylight, the squid's lights are seen as dark spots around its eyes and on the tips of the two longest tentacles that are attached to

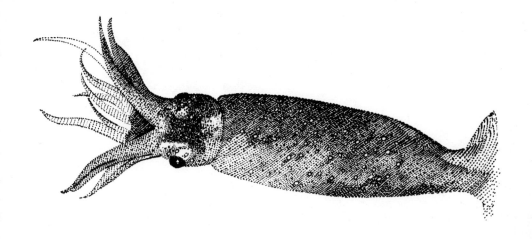

its head, as well as scattered over its body. In nighttime, however, the dark skin is pulled back from these areas, allowing bluish-white light to shine out. The squid's lanterns and those of other luminescent sea animals are called "photophores," from the Greek, meaning *light bearer*. The photophores, like flashlights, have built-in lenses to focus the light and reflectors to cast it out.

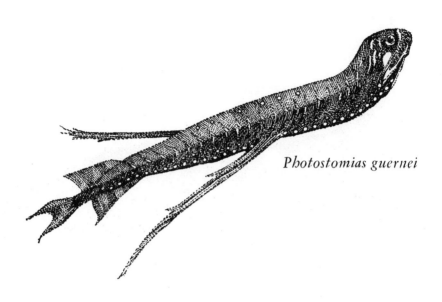

Photostomias guernei

The Twilight Zone

Down in the sea's depths, where sunlight
fades away, is the twilight zone. Many of the
fishes and many of the various squids that live
there light up. Their photophores shine in
lilac, purple-orange, yellow, and yellow-green,
but the most common colors are blue and blue-
green. A light meter lowered 900 feet into the
sea revealed more light at night from these

animals than is otherwise present during the day from the little sunlight that filters down.

Most fishes that flash in the deep are small, about six inches or less in length. They are strange looking, with sharp-fanged teeth, gaping mouths, upward-staring eyes, and odd parts hanging from their small bodies. These fierce, carnivorous predators feed on one another

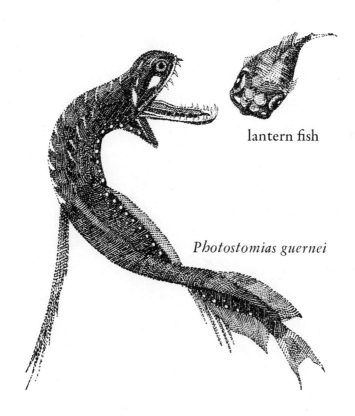

lantern fish

Photostomias guernei

and seem like weird creatures of the imagination compared to the commonly known fishes.

For ages, scientists thought that no life existed in the depths of the sea, that it was simply a dead, dark, cold, and empty wasteland. But in the early 1930's, a courageous American marine biologist, Charles William Beebe, opened up this mysterious underwater world. Beebe used a large steel globe, built to resist great pressures, to descend into the sea near the island of Bermuda. This globe, or bathysphere, was lowered on a long cable from a ship on the surface. The bathysphere had clear, quartz windows, searchlights, and telephones with which to communicate with the surface.

As Beebe descended, he observed changes in color due to the fading sunlight. Reds faded away at a depth of 20 feet, so that below that level scarlet shrimps, for example, did not appear red at all but instead looked black. The

color orange disappeared at 150 feet, yellow at 300 feet, and most all other colors were absent at 800 feet. Only blue and blue-black prevailed.

Below 400 feet no plants exist and food is scarce, since there is not sufficient light for making food. Some of it drifts down from above. Yet many animals, such as fishes, squids,

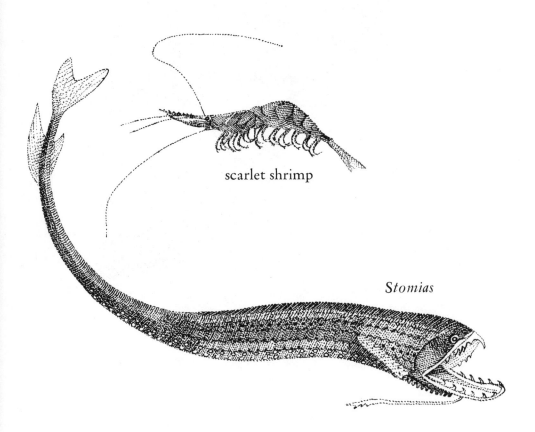

scarlet shrimp

Stomias

shrimps, and copepods (tiny crustaceans), make long upward journeys to the surface at night to find food. Survival is difficult. Each creature is prey for another.

Even though these animals have excellent eyes, seeing in the dark depths is difficult. Light is very useful. Thus, the greatest amount of bio-

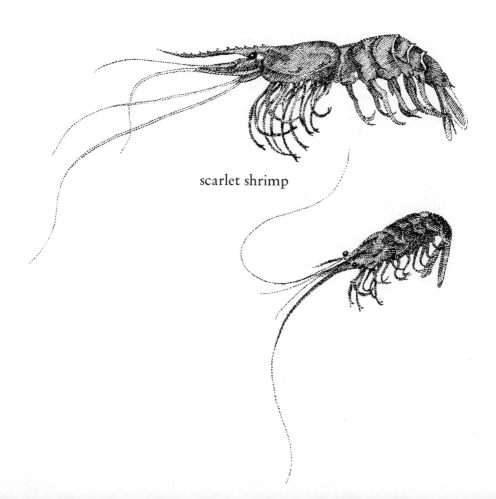

scarlet shrimp

luminescence is found between 750 and 2500 feet below the surface. There also, in the dark, cold twilight zone of intense pressure, most life in the depths exists.

The small lantern fishes light their way through the dark using two white headlights that emit beams perhaps a foot long. They shine as well from lights all over their body and even from tiny lanterns on their tongue. These body lights help to attract prey. They also may be used by lantern fishes of the same species to recognize each other for mating. One species of lantern, for example, has three rows of lights on its abdomen, while another has two. Not only can different species be recognized in the dark by their pattern of lights, males can be distinguished from females. A male lantern's lights are on top of his tail and are bright, while the female's are located beneath her tail and are dimmer.

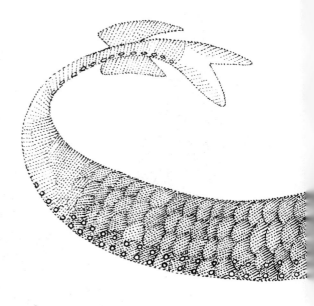

The slender, silvery viperfish, like the lantern fish, has large lights near its eyes. They may shine either with a steady or a flickering beam. As many as 350 lights line the roof of the viper-fish's mouth. This fearsome trap attracts prey when opened. It can expand like the mouth of a snake or a viper in order to engulf fish and shrimp almost as large as the viperfish itself.

Living far down in this region is a fish that fishes for its food. It is the angler fish. At the tip of a spine on its back is a light that the angler uses as a fishing lure. When prey is attracted by the light, the angler leads the victim before its waiting mouth and seizes it.

Another oddity about the deep-sea angler is that only the females have lights among all but two of some ninety species. Certain males, which live at great depths, have overcome this disadvantage of being lightless by finding a suitable female host and attaching themselves to her. They bite into her flesh and hold on for life, drawing food from her body. These males, merely six inches long, are much smaller than the female, which may measure up to a yard. In return for his food, the male supplies sperm when the female is ready to lay her eggs. Sometimes as many as three male anglers may attach themselves to a single female.

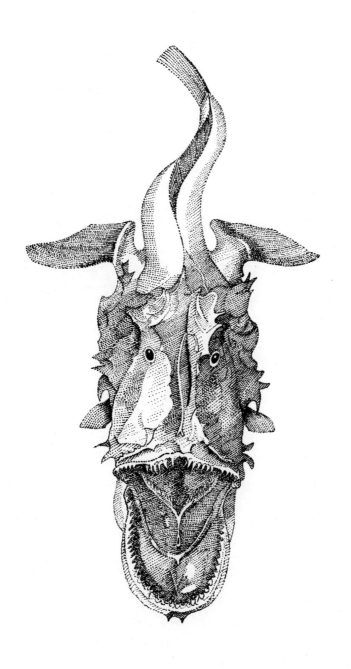

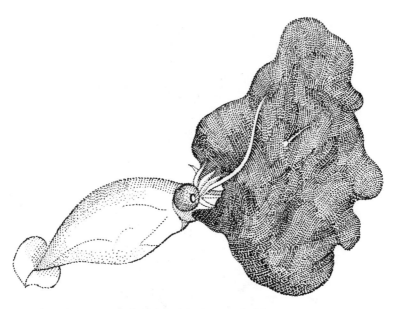

squid emitting a defensive luminous fluid

Besides helping various sea creatures find food and assisting them in reproduction, bioluminescence may aid some in yet another way: escaping from danger. Certain species of squid and shrimp, too, emit clouds of luminous fluid that dazzle, distract, and divert their enemies, while they race away to safety.

The small, silvery hatchetfish, so-called because its thin body is shaped like a hatchet blade, lives nearer the surface of the twilight zone and uses light in a different way: to hide. Organs along its sides and on its abdomen emit light which blends with that from above, camouflaging the hatchetfish from hungry predators below.

Near the Surface

Other fishes that live near the surface, or not far under it, including some types of sharks, are also thought to use their lights for hiding. Perhaps none is more unusual than the pony fish. This resident of the warm waters of the Indian and Pacific Oceans has a snout resembling the shape of a pony's head. It, too, has a bluish-white light along its abdomen, and it blends with light from the surface.

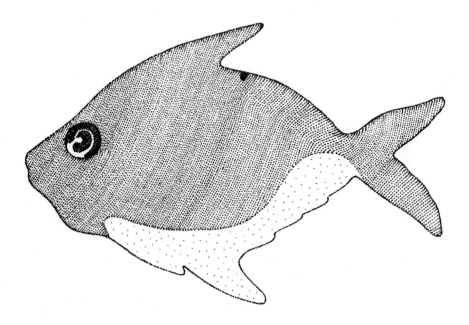

The pony fish, however, does not produce its own light. Glowing luminous bacteria live in a cone-shaped organ in its abdomen. This relationship between the fish and the bacteria is an example of symbiosis, that extraordinary arrangement in nature where two entirely different creatures live together for their mutual benefit. In this particular partnership, the pony fish benefits from the concealing light while the bacteria receive a good home and nourishment.

The pony fish has perfected the use of its light to a remarkable degree. At night, or when it wishes to descend to a depth where its light would ordinarily attract enemies, it shades it. It does so by means of a tissue that is stretched over the head of the light organ, covering and hiding the light. This technique enables the pony fish to adjust continually and blend into its background.

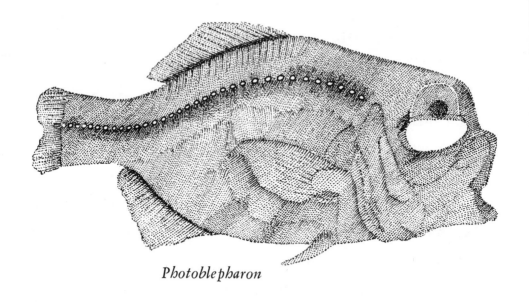

Photoblepharon

A number of fishes have bacterial lanterns and unusual shading devices. In the shallow waters of the Banda Sea off Indonesia, two are found. They are *Photoblepharon,* which means *light eyelid,* and *Anomalops,* which means *irregular eye.* Both fishes have a single, white, oval light organ under each eye. When *Photoblepharon* doesn't want its bluish-white light to shine through, it raises a dark eyelid up over the organ like a window shade. *Anomalops* conceals its light by rotating the entire organ into a special pocket of black tissue. These fishes are thought to use their lights to search with and perhaps also to lure and attract prey. Native fishermen actually cut out *Photoblepharon's* light organ and tie it to their fishing lines as bait. It is said to shine for about eight hours.

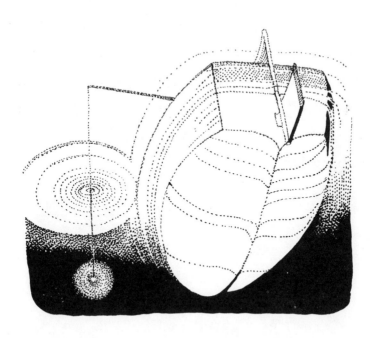

In Freshwater

Although there are numerous creatures in the sea that light up, only one bioluminescent freshwater animal is known thus far. It is a small black snail, the size of a raisin, which clings to stones and feeds on algae in the fast-moving brooks and rivers of New Zealand. This snail, known as *Latia,* has been studied thoroughly by scientists and found to produce its own green light. Whenever scientists discover new luminescent organisms, they try to determine whether the creature produces light itself, as *Latia* was found to do, or merely is a host to luminous bacteria, those tiny microscopic plants.

LUMINESCENT PLANTS

Bacteria

Among the plants, only the bacteria and the fungi, in addition to the dinoflagellates, produce light. Bacteria are thought to be the tiniest luminescent organisms. Some measure 1/20,000 of an inch and can be seen separately only under a microscope. Millions of luminescent bacteria must be present for their glow to be seen. The light does not flicker. It shines steadily all the time, night and day.

In the ancient world, the great Greek scientist, Aristotle, who lived in the fourth century B.C., described the bioluminescence produced by bacteria. He wrote about meat stored in peoples' homes "gleaming," and he commented that he had observed dead fish on beaches "glowing." In his book *De Sensu,* Aristotle wrote, "It is the nature of smooth things to shine in the dark as the heads of certain fishes. . . ." Aristotle could not have known in those days before microscopes that bacteria living on the flesh actually caused the light.

Luminous bacteria are probably responsible for many a legend and spooky tale of ghosts and spirits. The glow they produce on corpses is eerie and frightening. Imagine a whole battlefield alight with bodies of the dead and wounded.

Before the use of antiseptics, agents such as iodine that kill bacteria, luminous bacteria would frequently appear in the wounds of patients. Doctors in the 1860's, during the American Civil War, reported that their patients' wounds would sometimes show a dull light in the dark. This sight was considered a good sign, for luminescent wounds seemed to heal better and faster than those that were not. The luminous bacteria were not harmful. They helped remove dead tissues that otherwise might have provided food for disease-causing germs.

Luminous bacteria on food are not harmful either. They appear before spoilage. In 1889, a German university student named Tollhausen proved this fact with an unusual experiment that was recorded in his university thesis. He

prepared a broth of luminous bacteria. A cautious fellow, Tollhausen fed the preparation first to his cat. The cat remained well, so Tollhausen then added luminous bacteria to his own food for three days. He remained well too.

As Tollhausen found, luminous bacteria are not difficult to grow. They can be cultured easily in salt water with nutrients added. A French scientist, Raphael Dubois, created quite a spectacle at the Paris International Exposition of 1900 with luminescent bacteria. Dubois used large glass flasks filled with them to set a whole room aglow. The blue-green light was bright enough, even at night, so that people could read newspapers in it.

Fungi

The third group of plants that glow are the fungi, which include mushrooms and toad-

mushroom (*Pleurotus lampas*) by night

stools. In dark, damp, wooded places, dead
and rotting tree trunks, branches, and piles
of decaying wood may gleam with an eerie,
steady, dull yellow or green light. In many
places this glow is called fox fire and is considered mystical and magical. The fungi that
produce the light are very simple plants. They
lack chlorophyl, the green coloring substance
that enables more highly developed plants to

carry on photosynthesis and make their own food. These fungi take their nourishment from wood by penetrating it with fine threadlike roots called "mycelia." Because of the fungi, the wood appears to glow. Luminescent mushrooms may glow from the roots, the cap, or the entire plant. During the Second World War, an American reporter on the island of New Guinea in the South Pacific told of writing a letter home to his wife by the light of five mushrooms.

THE MYSTERY OF BIOLUMINESCENCE

Origins

Mushrooms light up. Certain bacteria glow. Tiny one-celled organisms in the sea flash. How does luminescence serve these creatures? Similar organisms seem to survive quite successfully without this characteristic. Even when nature's light obviously helps some animals to mate, find food, or avoid enemies, did it originate for these purposes? Or was luminescence already present, and use then found for it? Answers to these questions have been sought by many scientists. Clues have been found in the history of the earth and its changing conditions; bioluminescent creatures have been collected and studied. Still, research through experimentation continues. Much has been learned, but many theories also have been tested and discarded. The true nature and function of bioluminescence remain largely a mystery.

Old Notions

Before the modern era, people thought that tree trunks glowed because they were enchanted or possessed with magic. In Italy, fireflies were once believed to shine with the spirits of the dead. Scientifically minded people believed that sea light at night was the result of heat absorbed by the water during the day. Others held that it came somehow from the oily slime of fishes. The American statesman and scientist, Benjamin Franklin, once reasoned that the phosphorescence of the sea was caused by friction between waves and the air.

Superstitions and other old notions have gradually given way through the years to scientific knowledge developed by observation and experimentation. Aristotle, centuries ago, provided the important observation that nature's lights are cold. They "are not in their nature fire nor any species of fire, yet seem to produce light." Hold a firefly by its tail, and you will find that its lights are heatless unlike the ordinary lighted electric bulb. Electricity uses heat to make light and is inefficient. It produces about 90 percent heat and only 10 percent light. But firefly light is chemical and efficient. It is almost 100 percent pure light.

Experiments

Late in the seventeenth century, the English chemist, Robert Boyle, made an important scientific discovery about bioluminescence. Boyle placed pieces of shining wood, meat, and fish under glass bell jars and observed, as he pumped air out, that his specimens stopped glowing. When he pumped air back in, they shined once again. Boyle had learned that living things use air, actually oxygen, to light up.

In 1885, more than two hundred years after Boyle's discovery, another important development occurred. Raphael Dubois in his laboratory at Tamaris-sur-Mer in France experimented with *Pyrophorus,* the fire beetle. Dubois separated and ground up the two light organs from the beetle. He mixed one with cold water. This solution glowed for some minutes and then went out. It seemed that whatever caused the light had been used up. He mixed the other light organ

68

Robert Boyle

with hot water. This solution did not glow at all even after it cooled. Heat apparently destroyed whatever produced the light. Dubois now mixed the cold solution that no longer glowed with the heated solution that never had glowed. To his amazement, the combined solution lighted. But why?

Dubois repeated the experiment many times. Later he substituted the luminous juice of a clam for the light organs of the fire beetle, called *Pholas dactylus,* which shines with blue light in five places on its body. Dubois had the same results with the clam as he had with the beetle. He began to think that besides oxygen, there must be at least two substances, or chemicals, responsible for the light. Something in the cold-water solution had been used up by the time the light went out. We'll call it Substance A. Something else in it, however, was still good. We'll call it Substance B. In the hot-

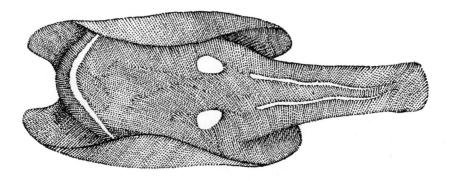

clam (*Pholas dactylus*)

water solution, Substance A had not been used up at all and was still good, but Substance B had been destroyed. By combining the two solutions, both necessary chemicals were united and light was produced.

Dubois named the chemical unaffected by heat luciferin (Substance A). Lucifer in Latin means *bearer of light.* The chemical destroyed by heat, he called luciferase (Substance B).

He used the *ase* ending with this name to indicate that he thought the chemical was an enzyme. Enzymes are agents easily destroyed by heat. They cause chemical changes without being used up themselves. The discovery by Dubois that nature's light is produced by a chemical acted upon by an enzyme aided other scientists in their research. It gave them a model for further work. One of these scientists was the American biologist, E. Newton Harvey.

Doctor Harvey, studying bioluminescence at Princeton University, received from Dubois a thoughtful gift of luminescent material. Harvey and his wife Ethel, also a biologist, devoted the next forty years to studying nature's light. With the help of other young scientists, Harvey described and classified all known bioluminescent organisms and wrote many books on the subject. He worked with fireflies, the fireworm, and luminescent shrimp, but his

crustacean (*Cypridina*)

major efforts were with the tiny crustacean *Cypridina* from Japan. *Cypridina,* he found, produces bright blue light in the sea by secreting luciferin and luciferase made by separate glands in its body.

Doctor Harvey's investigation showed that each organism produced its own special lighting chemicals. The luciferin and luciferase of fire-flies, for example, differ from those of lumines-cent shrimp. Light cannot be obtained usually by combining the luciferin from one kind of creature with the luciferase of another. They do not fit together chemically to produce light any more than pieces from different puzzles fit together to form a picture.

The chemistry of nature's light continued to interest a number of scientists around the world, but bioluminescence remained largely a curiosity until a remarkable discovery in 1946 by the outstanding scientist, Doctor William McElroy. At Johns Hopkins University, McElroy set out to learn what causes differences in the brightness of firefly light. He decided to test the chemical adenosine triphosphate, or ATP, on the firefly system and found that it had an exciting effect. Then, using thousands of firefly tails, he man-aged to obtain not only pure extracts of luciferin and luciferase, but also, as he expected, he discovered the presence of ATP and extracted it.

McElroy prepared mixtures of luciferin and luciferase in four small glass Petri dishes. He then added ATP to each one in increasing amounts. The first solution, with little ATP, had a dull greenish-yellow glow. The next was somewhat brighter. The last two solutions, with the most ATP, shone a bright yellow. The chemical ATP, McElroy found, is what controls the brightness of firefly light. McElroy's discovery had far-reaching applications.

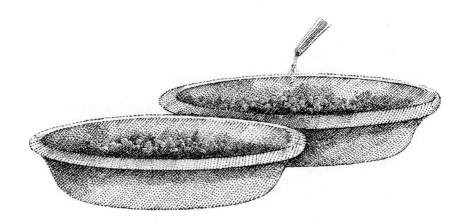

ATP is the important energy-carrying molecule present in every living cell. It is basic to all life processes. It provides the energy for growth, for healing, and for work. It enables us to think, to act, to turn the pages of this book. McElroy's discovery that ATP controls the brightness of firefly light gave scientists a new, quick, and useful tool for investigating life itself. With ATP removed, firefly extract becomes a means to test for the presence of ATP.

McElroy's research required millions of fireflies. But how to obtain them? He placed an advertisement in a Baltimore, Maryland, newspaper in 1948, offering a bounty for fireflies brought to his laboratory in good condition. A reward of twenty-five cents was offered for every 100 fireflies, and a bonus of ten dollars was promised to the person who brought in the most. Boys and girls started spending their summer evenings catching fireflies. So began an annual firefly collection campaign that has continued for many years with youngsters in other parts of the United States joining in. As many as 800,000 fireflies were gathered in one summer. In 1961, scientists at Hopkins learned how to synthesize, to manufacture chemically, firefly luciferin. Live fireflies, however, are still needed to provide luciferase.

SCIENCE USES BIOLUMINESCENCE

In Medicine

Firefly extract is playing an increasingly important role today in scientific research. Its luminescent reaction to ATP is becoming a valuable aid to diagnosis in medicine. With ATP removed, firefly extract will light up when placed on healthy body cells because they supply sufficient ATP. Less light is produced, however, when the extract is added to cancer cells, because these cells have little ATP. This difference in light gives an accurate, speedy method for cancer detection.

Other bioluminescent organisms have been found to be sensitive to other substances, and they will react when they come in contact with them. The sticky, blue-green slime of a small, odd-looking marine worm lights up in the presence of iron. The paddle worm, four inches long, looks like pieces of macaroni strung together. It lives in a U-shaped tube in the ocean bottom and paddles water with its middle sections. This behavior is the source of its name. The paddle worm also is helpful to medical scientists.

Adequate amounts of iron are necessary to our health. Too little causes anemia, a condition that weakens us. Paddle-worm extract enables scientists to check the amount of iron in our blood to diagnose anemia. This test is so useful that chemists are trying to copy the paddle worm and make its extract artificially. They believe that it may contain a single special lighting chemical called a "photoprotein," in which the luciferin and luciferase are joined together as one.

The jellyfish, *Aequorea,* is also thought to use a single photoprotein to luminesce. *Aequorea* is the only organism known to require calcium for its bioluminescent reaction. Lights rimming its dome will glow when they come in contact with this mineral, which we need for strong teeth and bones. Like iron, too much or too little calcium also causes serious health problems. Extracts of *Aequorea,* called "aequorin," provide an accurate means of measuring calcium levels in the blood. Scientists, however, must wait until summertime, when the jellyfish is plentiful,

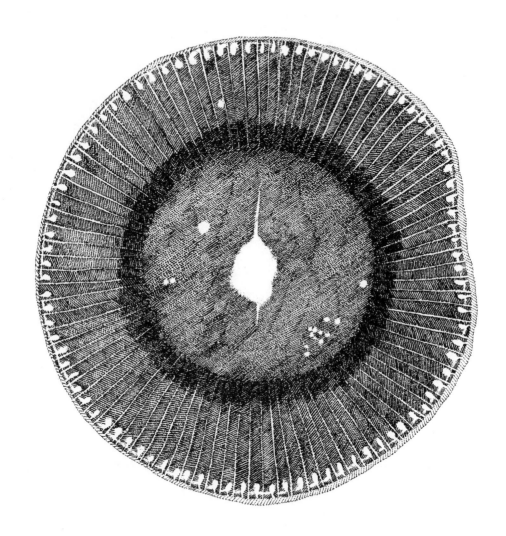

jellyfish (*Aequorea*)

in order to net it off the western coasts of the United States and Canada.

Once caught, the jellyfish's little lights must be removed to obtain the extract. This bothersome and tedious task was done by hand with a scissors, until in 1969 a machine was invented for the purpose. Would you think that ten tons of jellyfish would yield only 1/200 of an ounce of aequorin? This small yield has encouraged scientists to try to make the substance artificially.

Aequorin is valuable, too, because it lights up in the presence of strontium. Radioactive strontium is a dangerous product of atomic explosions, and aequorin detects it.

In Drug and Explosive Detection

An ingenious application of bioluminescence to help solve a difficult current problem involves the use of luminous bacteria. Strains of these

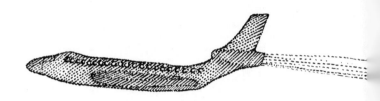

organisms taken from the sea have been found to glow in the presence of marijuana and narcotics such as heroin and cocaine. They react in the same way also to explosives like dynamite. Freeze-dried, these bacteria become part of a small portable detector about the size of a cigar box that customs and security officers can use at airports and harbors.

In Pollution Control

Bioluminescent materials are also helping to safeguard the quality of the air we breathe and the purity of the water we drink. Luciferin

and luciferase from the tiny *Cypridina,* when exposed to pollutants from jet fuels, become inactive and unable to light up. *Cypridina,* therefore, can signal when our air is clean and warn us when it is polluted. This test is so sensitive that *Cypridina* may be used to protect

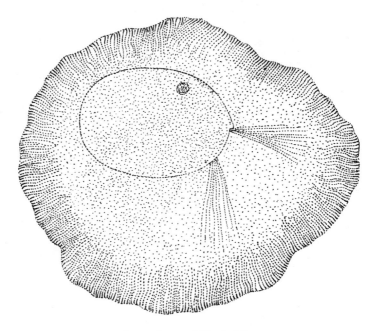

a close view of *Cypridina*

our astronauts from fuel contaminants in space vehicles.

Since firefly extract lights up in the presence of ATP, it gives us a means to detect harmful bacteria in our drinking water. Safe water has few or no germs, and firefly extract will not light up in it. Waters polluted by sewage are rich in bacteria, which contain ATP. This impure, unsafe water will cause samples of firefly extract to glow.

In Conservation

Scientists concerned with the depletion of life in the sea are also using bioluminescence in their researches. The United States National Marine Fisheries Service has been using special television cameras to record the movements of schools of fish. An airborne camera, especially sensitive to light of low intensities, photographs fish at night in the light produced by dino-

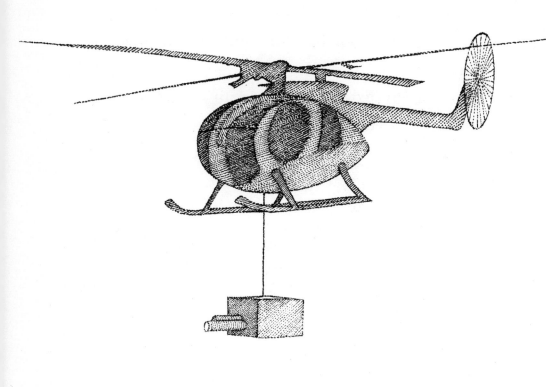
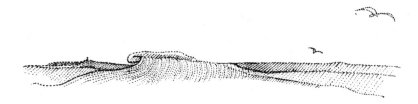

flagellates. Another kind of television camera is lowered into the sea and sends pictures up to a laboratory ashore. It is hoped that these studies may help fishery scientists to determine the location, distribution, and numbers of various fish populations and, thereby, benefit our efforts to conserve marine life.

In the future bioluminescent creatures may precede man into outer space. A clam or a firefly could well be the first living animal to test the atmosphere of a distant planet.

Nature's light sparking in the sea, glowing on the land, and twinkling in the night air has stirred man's curiosity since ancient times. His desire to find out what caused it led him to probe the mysteries of bioluminescence. In this instance as in many others, the pursuit of knowledge for its own sake, not for any practical reason, has produced a great discovery.

GLOSSARY

Adenosine triphosphate (ATP)—the chemical formed in living cells that supplies energy for the processes of life

Algae (Alga, singular)—simple plants that lack roots, stems, and leaves; they range from one-celled forms, microscopic in size, to multicellular forms, such as giant seaweeds hundreds of feet in length

Bathysphere—a submersible globe employed by scientists to observe deep-sea marine life

Bioluminescence—heatless light produced by chemical means in living organisms

Carnivorous — flesh-eating (carnivorous animals are those that feed principally upon other animals)

Chlorophyll — the green coloring matter in plants essential to the manufacture of food

Copepods — certain crustaceans, usually minute; together with tiny plants they form a major part of the food chain in the sea

Crustaceans — a group of animals, mainly aquatic, such as shrimps, lobsters, crabs, copepods, and others possessing hard external shells and jointed limbs

Dinoflagellate — a one-celled organism with two whiplike tails, chiefly marine; some are bioluminescent

Enzyme — a chemical produced by living cells that causes other chemicals to react

Luciferase — an enzyme that causes luciferin to react with oxygen to produce light

Luciferin — a substance found in certain living organisms capable of reacting with oxygen to produce bioluminescence

Mycelium (Mycelia, plural) — that part of a fungus, consisting of fine threadlike branches, which enables the fungus to penetrate and extract nourishment from the matter upon which it lives

Photophore — the organ in certain fishes, crustaceans, and squids where light is produced

Photoprotein — a single lighting chemical in which luciferin and luciferase may be joined together

Predator — an animal that hunts and eats other animals

Symbiosis — an arrangement in nature where two different organisms live together, often for their mutual benefit

Synthesize — to combine separate parts or elements to form a substance; scientists study natural materials to discover their chemical parts in order to reproduce or *synthesize* them in the laboratory

Twilight zone — that area in the sea depths where sunlight barely reaches, about 750 to 2500 feet below the surface

INDEX

indicates illustrations

95